The Electric Oracle Speaks
Wisdom Now And Forever

ROLLAND E. PROULX

da
PRESS

TORONTO, CANADA

The Electric Oracle Speaks
Wisdom Now And Forever
by Rolland E. Proulx

Copyright © 2004 Rolland E. Proulx
Published by daPress
599-B Yonge Street, Suite 221, Toronto, Ontario M4Y 1Z4
dapress@rollandproulx.com
Distributed in Canada and the United States by Hushion
House Publishing Limited

ISBN-0-9735717-0-5

Cover design and art illustrations © 2004 Rolland E. Proulx
Photograph of the author by Sharon Singer

Printed in Canada

DEDICATION

For R.H.H.
Armand & Leontine Proulx

Best wishes

Robert D. Proulx

ACKNOWLEDGEMENTS

Where to begin? There are many who have helped and encouraged me directly and indirectly in realizing my first of many books.

Many thanks to Shane Nagel and Andrew Faroutani for their generous support throughout this process.

A special thank you to Sharon Singer, Christian Singer and Alan Gatschene for their valuable suggestions, ideas and encouragement.

Big thanks to my supportive computer wizard friend, Robert Whitton, for saving the day and keeping the computer in working order.

My gratitude goes out to Raul Regalado for his superb editing skills and QuarkXPress expertise.

To my dear friend Herb Maton, a singular thanks for his unending loyalty and for generously letting me share his computer over an extended period of time while liberally pouring tea and serving up cookies *sans fin*. Let's not forget Missy (Herb's cat) for her loving disposition and for just being there.

Last but not least my heartfelt gratitude goes to Arthur Clark for his unswerving support, fidelity and for believing in me.

THE ELECTRIC ORACLE SPEAKS

TABLE OF CONTENTS

INTRODUCTION

The idea for *The Electrical Oracle Speaks* came to me three years ago. Writing and getting the book into print has been a veritable saga, a mother of a process, an incredible time of learning and discovery. It is rather interesting that from the moment I started working on this book I entered a cycle of drastic change that was to turn my world upside-down and last until the present time. The source of the universe was giving me an opportunity to put into practice what I was writing about. Everything was urging me to let go of the past, offering me numerous challenges for self-renewal whilst stoking the fires of self-transformation. If there was ever a time to apply the *transformative power of positive thinking,* this was it.

My vision for this book was to provide encouragement to those who need it most (and don't we all?) to inspire people to recognize and trust their abilities while providing ideas for self-change that are practical and viable. The inspiration for this book is based on the power of thought—thoughts are things and thoughts control our lives. This is a *you can do it, go for it* book filled with memorable sayings that help readers deal with everyday existence and provide answers that can easily be called upon in difficult times. The other important thing for me was that the book be aesthetically pleasing and a joy to behold.

The order in which aphorisms appear in the book was intended to create an intuitive mood as opposed to a logical sequence: an eclectic combination of sayings, insights and illustrations that speak to the reader in a personal way. In short, *The Electric Oracle Speaks* is a little breath of the positive in an ailing world, a reminder to remember, not to forget, what really matters in this life.

Dare To Be

Part One
APHORISMS

There is
a solution to
every problem.
The challenge
is in being
open to the
solution.

If at first
you don't
succeed, fall
apart, have a
breakdown.
After all,
you're perfect.

Mistakes
are often
the precursors
to great
discoveries.

Your thoughts
can beat you
into the ground
or become
wings to
soar with.

Impossible
is a state
of mind.
Change it.

Two and two
make five.
It's the hidden
factor you
forgot to add.

Put nothing
into what
you do and get
nothing.

An action is better than no action.

One step
at a time
walks the walk.

Stretch your body, your thoughts and your imagination. Dare to be original.

Degrees
and money
do not
a thinker make.

13

Poverty
is not the enemy
of creativity
and inventiveness.
Comfort is.

Question
everything
and everyone.
No one person
or group has
all the answers.

Questions are a sign of intelligence at work.

16

When you solicit
other people's
opinions and
advice, more
than likely you're
getting their
limitations.

Life is like
walking a
tightrope—
balance,
balance,
balance.

Keep one eye
on the stars
and one
on the ground;
that way you can
dream without
stumbling.

It's not what
happens to you
that matters.
It's how you
react to what
is happening
that is critical.

Forgive,
and you release
yourself from
bondage.

The past
is the past.
Fini,
gone,
done with.
Move on.

Bad attitudes
make for
a bumpy ride.

Thought is
the builder.
What you
habitually think,
you become.

You can
do more than
one thing well.

25

Don't put down what you fail to understand.

Magnanimity gives the benefit of the doubt to others.

Coincidence?
I think not.

Too often
we punish
ourselves for
not being what
we think we
should be.
What is wrong
with being you?

Applause seeking: After all the approval-seeking antics, the only thing you're left with is exhaustion.

30

I can't
means
I don't want to.

Better to possess things than to be possessed by them.

Sympathy
is nothing but
empty babble.
Action talks.

Mirror, mirror on the wall, who is the most beautiful of them all? The real self, not the faux image you're projecting.

True love is
unconditional.
It does not seek
payback.

Blame
is blind
to itself.

Knowledge without wisdom is **frightening.**

Negative
past fixations
create miserable
hotbeds
of disease
and misery.

Give from
your heart and
expect nothing in
return. That way
we won't have to
listen to that tired
old song *after all I
did for you*.

39

Rewards
are for pets
who do
neat tricks.

The benefits
of an open mind
are no less than
miraculous.

Patience is about knowledge and timing. Timing is everything.

Suffering
purifies
the spirit.

The body is intelligent. Talk to it.

Your thoughts
dictate your life.
Mind your
thoughts.

Doubt
is an insidious
worm.
Step on it.

Do you have
a chip on your
shoulder?
The weight
is affecting
your gait.

When you belittle others you're busy putting yourself down.

The biggest
limitations
in your life
are the ones
you set.

Don't ask from a rock what a tree can give you.

Fear
has a way
of complicating
things.

You only live once. NOT!

Asking everyone's opinion makes for confusion.

Welcome the unusual into your life.

The greatest
obstacle to
your happiness
is yourself.

Treat all
living things
respectfully—
you included.

Life
is a constant
series of
new beginnings.
Spirit renewal
knows no age.

Unity
is not all
looking
and thinking
alike.

Karma
is the law
of cause
and effect
in action—
not punishment.

An argument
is brown ego-dirt
mucking up
the atmosphere.
Walk away.

Are you
holding onto
belief systems
you've never
questioned?
Chances are
they are
not your own.

Go the extra mile
and give a little
more than
is expected
of you.

Selfless service
to others is
the fastest way to
God consciousness.
No fees,
no degrees.

If you think
you are only
your body
then you are
nobody.

I bow to you.
By thy God.

What you imagine the afterlife to be affects it.

Instead of
rest in peace
it is better
to wish those
who are leaving
this incarnation
Godspeed.

If there
is no rest
for the wicked
then the good
need to get
busy.

There is
no death—
only constant
transformation.

Beauty is a manifestation of positive energy at work.

Surround yourself with beautiful things. It will do wonders for your consciousness.

Spiritual commitment is everything. It's the stuff of heroes.

Get a rest from
the mind-chatter.
Meditate.

Listen
to your
inner voice.
You might learn
something and
spare yourself
a bunch
of grief.

Do you believe in retirement? Cul-de-sac.

Imagine
the so-called
unimaginable.
Reach out
beyond the limits
of your imaginary
limitations.

Forget
newspapers,
television
and radio
for a few days
and marvel at
what you
didn't miss.

Everyone
has a purpose
and you
do make
a difference
in this world.

Life
is an incredible
opportunity
begging to be
lived.

Don't be shy. Express your gratitude whenever the opportunity arises.

Forget your woes and get busy counting your blessings.

It's not
the form you
create that
counts—
it's the quality of
the energy you
put into it.

The heart
never lies. The
rational mind
does.

Truth
belongs to
everyone.
Trust yourself
and listen
to your heart.

84

You can't
compare
diamonds
to pearls, so
why compare
yourself
to others?

Work
on yourself.
That will
keep you busy
for a few
lifetimes.

Patience
is not
waiting around—
it's foresight.

Don't be a miser. Let your enthusiasm shine.

Conventional thinking is a dead end.

What was
good enough for
your grandparents
and parents
may not be
good enough for
you. Think for
yourself.

90

Today
builds tomorrow.
Live in the *now*
and think *future*.

91

Self-transformation is a turn-on.

If you blame
everyone
and everything
for your life woes,
then run to the
nearest mirror
and face
the perpetrator.

It is foolish
to judge and
condemn others;
after all,
you may have
been or will be
in their shoes in
another lifetime.

Every time
you seek
approval
you develop
a power leak.

Make this world
a better place
for one person
and your life
has not
been in vain.

The future
is through
cooperation
and
personal striving.

Competition smacks of approval-seeking.

Encourage
rather than
discourage.
Be magnanimous.

Forgive.
It's heroic.

Mother Earth
is a living,
breathing entity.
She is not
very happy
with us
at present.

When you think you have it all then you don't.

The definition
of hardcore
karma: family.

If at first
you don't
succeed,
sit down
and carefully
examine your
thought patterns.

Check your beliefs systems closely for they may harbour cesspools of negativity.

Freedom requires of you the utmost responsibility.

Regret
is a dirty word.
Admit your
mistakes
and then
move on.

107

Don't
worry yourself
with others'
shortcomings.
After all,
you have enough
of your own
to deal with.

The road to hell
is not only paved
with good
intentions—
it is absolutely
littered with
do-good
abominations.

Ego:
Controller
extraodinaire.

Part Two

ORACLE

OBSERVATIONS

ORACLE OBSERVATIONS: ONE
BELIEVE IN YOURSELF

Too often we punish ourselves for not being what we think we should be.

Believe in yourself and others believe in you—not vice-versa. Confidence has a magic of its own. Like a magnet it draws positive forces into life and attracts a wide array of possibilities. Confidence is a *yes to life, I can do it* word. The opposite holds true for negative thinking. It tends to repulse and block the flow of opportunities attracting an assortment of no good. It screams *I am worthless*. The effects of little or no confidence are astounding: expect low self-esteem, doubt, self-pity, and ill health. The repercussions of sporting a self-defeating attitude are horrendous.

A popular pastime is punishing yourself for not being what you think you should be. Add beating yourself up for not fulfilling someone else's expectations, and if that is not enough, throw in guilt for letting them down. Parents too often interfere with the natural development of their children, weighing them down with selfish wish lists and demands that only serve to confuse and undermine their offsprings' purpose in life. The scary part is what parents imagine being in the best interest of their loved ones, like *you should be a lawyer, you should marry and have children,* etc. I like to think of it as mom and dad's guide to running or ruining your life. Nobody has the right to interfere with your development, not even a well-meaning parent. By the way, when you hear yourself saying *I should do this,* remember it's not your voice talking.

It is a far better, healthier and more constructive choice to let go of what you think you're supposed to do in life and get on with what you want to do. The consequence of not doing your thing is damaging and far-reaching in the long run. Bear in mind nobody has the right to get in the way of your true path. Your way is unique to you and deep down you know what is

right for you. Trust in your feelings, in what you do know, and act accordingly with confidence. The rest will come.

The sooner you accept and approve of yourself, warts and all, the less time you will waste seeking approval from one and all. Instead, put your time into exploring your inimitable abilities and talents. No two persons are alike; every person has something singular to offer this world. Dare to respect your ideas, dare to believe in your work and fearlessly believe in yourself. The only thing you have to lose is your fear. Give yourself the love you need, be kind to yourself and follow your inner voice. Now is a good time to begin.

115

Aim High

Oracle Observations: Two
Forgive, Forget and Forge Ahead

Forgive. Free yourself from bondage.

To forgive or not to forgive—that is the question. The obvious answer is to forgive, though this seems to elude countless people. Everything about forgiving is about you. It's not really about the person who has wronged you. The beauty of forgiving is that it releases you from the past, and that can only be good. You can get on with your life and live in the present, otherwise the past will only continue to devour precious energies that can be more effectively used in the here and now.

Many believe the act of forgiving means that whatever wrongs they experienced at the hands of another has now been made right, when in fact, the person has been absolved and not the act. Let's get real: there is nothing honorable about being unforgiving. This ugly scourge thrives on bitterness,

117

resentment and malice. Throw in hate, rage, and revenge. It's disheartening to think that this reckless and sad behavior can drag on for years. In the end the injured party will be the loser, nothing will have been solved and holding onto past hurts will only cause your wounds to fester. Self-punishment, anyone?

Life is experience. *It's not what happens to you that matters. It's how you react to what is happening that is critical.* We all know several persons who have been trapped in the victim hold for years. They never fail to let you know that they were abused, eager to recount sordid details of what happenned to them in the past; how the monster in question ruined their lives. The same story is repeated over and over again as though it happened yesterday.

The important thing to remember in life is that you always have a choice. You cannot change what happens to you, but you can change your reaction to the challenges at hand; therein lies your power point.

Blame does not heal the past. There is magic in the act of forgiving. This noble and heroic action frees you from bondage and empowers you to begin anew. The vital thing to keep in mind, in the ever present now is that everyday is a new beginning, and furthermore a generous quantity of new opportunities and posssibilites are forever in the making. The only thing the universe asks of you is that you be open and receptive and ready to change. So why not forge ahead and forget the past? You can do it.

Trust Your Intuition

ORACLE OBSERVATIONS: THREE
THINK POSITIVE

Positive thinking is expansive, energizing and empowering.

Imagine—you are constantly thinking, churning out causative thoughts that are actively shaping, influencing and affecting every aspect of your life. Picture this endless thought flow continually creating your future in the ever-present now.

What kind of thoughts are you putting out? Unfortunately, little consideration is given to the power of thought and its unforgiving influence. Thought is always in search of expression, seeking to materialize in one form or another according to the energy it has been saturated with. Basically, what you think is what you get. For instance, if you believe something is impossible to do then it will be so. You will have made it impossible. Whether you believe in the power of thought or not, you are consciously or unconsciously creating your own reality for better or worse, which means you are responsible for your thoughts and the consequences that ensue.

Positive thinking is not optimism, nor does it have anything to do with being wishful or hopeful. Positive thinking is consciously working with your thoughts in order to effect constructive changes that will benefit your life in an effective manner, which is both creative and liberating. Positive thinking calls for a hands-on approach; take responsibility for your thoughts. It is never too late to take back your power and revolutionize your life for the better if you choose to do so, provided you are steadfast, persevering and have a burning desire for self-renewal. This calls for a willingness to let go of the past, think for yourself and order your life in such a way that it will work for you and invite positive energies into your environment.

When you apply positive thinking, its expansive nature will open up a new cache of possibilities, energize your everyday life and inspire you to greater

heights. Whatever your current situation is, there is always a way for you to transform yourself for the better—make no mistake about this. Let nothing dissuade you in your quest for something greater and nobler. Know and believe with all your heart that you can and will succeed. Wrap yourself up in trust and faith and nothing can stand in your way to a successful, fulfilling and healthy life. Let's get positive.

123

Love Yourself

ORACLE OBSERVATIONS: FOUR
LISTEN TO YOUR INNER VOICE

There is no sense like sixth sense.

This is one know-it-all you may want to listen to—your intuition, that is. Intuition is a great time-saver, protector and all-around guide. Everyone has experienced this wonderful, awesome faculty. Intuition is that part of you that knows what you cannot intellectually or rationally perceive with the conscious mind. Call it what you want—gut feeling, hunch, straight or direct knowledge—intuition is an invaluable ally that can serve you well during your brief visit on planet Earth, provided of course that you acknowledge its existence and apply it in your everyday life.

Intuition works in its own beautiful way, unfettered by time, distance and logic. It talks to you in its unique language via visions, symbols, feelings and other means, always the faithful guide that can save you a lot

of trouble, if you take the time to listen.

Too often this fiery quality is scorned and rejected. Why deny, ridicule, doubt or simply dismiss that which is a vital part of you? Refusing to recognize intuition is like refusing to acknowledge that you can hear. Let's face it: the unforeseen makes up the greater part of life and because it is invisible doesn't imply that it is nonexistent. Some even fear this natural aptitude believing it to be spooky and creepy, thoughtlessly relegating intuition to some dark, nebulous sphere. Throughout the ages, intuition has been ignorantly denied, maligned and conveniently ascribed as the work of the Devil (I find it remarkable how this guy gets credit for so much that is positive and good in this world).

What better occasion to listen to what you intuit than during turbulent times such as this, when censorship is rampant, as well as unabashed propaganda and disinformation? Imagine this

negative force vying to control your life, trying to tell you what to think and how to live—no, thank you. It is much wiser to rely on your own sense of what is right or wrong and fearlessly trust your insight as to what is best for you.

Trust is the name of the game. Trust is the one requisite your sixth sense needs in order to develop, and the more you acknowledge it the better it will serve you. The greater your autonomy, the less fearful you are and the more empowered you will become. After all, whom are you to trust if you don't trust you?

127

Approve Of Yourself

ORACLE OBSERVATIONS: FIVE
DARE TO BE YOU

Comparing yourself to others puts you at a great disadvantage.

Oh what a wonderful life! So much to discover, explore and experience, one big opportunity waiting for you. Why limit yourself to a little corner of your being, when life offers so much and invites you to dream, dare and express yourself in all your matchless magnificence? The joy of experience beckons you to embrace life wholeheartedly and fearlessly. Surprisingly, this being said, there is a widespread propensity for holding back and playing it safe.

What is wrong with being you? Why not be the best that you can be instead of wasting time comparing yourself to others? Self-limitation is generally borne out of fear, and the causes are many and complex. For instance you may be holding onto old, outmoded belief systems that have nothing to do with your way of life and your generation. Or you may be conducting your life according to negative attitudes that you have unconsciously adopted and failed to detect or question. Then again, you may be holding back because you think others will reject you, or worse ridicule you. The fear of ridicule is probably one of the biggest reasons why people shy away and fail to give things a try.

Eventually, over time, the effects of limiting your self will begin to surface and the negative harvest that can be expected is not very exciting. Look forward to low self-esteem, depression, self-inflicted punishment and anger, even rage. Don't forget the inevitable specter of disease, possible addiction and poor relationships. This toxic cocktail tends to stir up a familiar negative side effect: blame. Blame the world, blame someone or something—but above all, avoid taking responsibility for yourself.

Everything changes when you boldly take responsibility for yourself. New empowering energies

are released, giving urge to greater strivings and providing you with the inner strength and incentive to actualize bigger and better achievements. It is never too late to change and now is always a good time to get realizing what you may have been putting off for a long time. The remarkable thing is that when you follow your own path, the amount of energy required to succeed is less than when you attempt to be something you are not. Trust yourself; work from within to without, and no matter what, steadfastly pursue your quest.

Bear in mind there will be opposition and criticism and sometimes out-and-out condemnation, especially from those who are dear and close to you. Doing your thing tends to evoke this negative reaction. Yet, always remember it is your life to live, your opportunity to experience with open arms the wealth, grandeur and beauty life has to offer. No one can live it for you, so go ahead—it's your party and you can laugh if you want to.

131

Accept Yourself

ORACLE OBSERVATIONS: SIX
NOTHING TO FEAR

Fear depletes, fearlessness replenishes.

The old adage *there is nothing to fear but fear itself* comes to mind. It might be more apropos to say *there is nothing to fear but your self.* Why? Because fear is a self-induced state; your own colored reaction, if you like, to whatever it is you dread. For instance, dogs may terrify you, even as others absolutely love them. Fear has a way of clouding the mind to the point of stretching and distorting reality, until any and all vestiges of common sense are wrung out, and all you are left with is a mere figment of your imagination. Unfortunately, what is imagined to be real will for the most part be projected onto others, which in turn might open a can of worms.

There can be no good from actions that are generated by fear. These powerful negative emotions, when fueled by denials, doubts, and suspicion-laden

thoughts, eventually grow and become the cause for innumerable desperate acts. For copious examples of fear-fueled reactions, check your local news media and tune into a world gone mad, a veritable pessimistic frenzy, fraught with hate, rage and other good-for-nothing effects.

The good news is there is nothing to fear, and fear can be conquered when right attitude and right thinking are brought into play. Positive thinking, together with faith and trust, will help you overcome negative emotions and thoughts. With a little effort you can consciously keep track of your thoughts and monitor the quality of what you are giving out. This way you will avoid untold difficulties and needless suffering as you go about freeing yourself from debilitating, erroneous thoughts. Gradually you will become more and more empowered and attract enhanced equanimity, health, and yes, even joy.

Always bear in mind that you are stronger and bigger then all your obstacles. Add perseverance plus steadfastness, and eventually you will conquer and overcome everything that is blocking your way. For some this may be hard to accept, yet obstacles are really blessings in disguise. Obstacles challenge your resolve and resourcefulness while testing your strength and courage, thereby creating through what you have experienced a whole new perspective on life. The positive outcome of this will empower and inspire you to greater heights. Victory is yours.

Finally, you may want to work with positive affirmations that affirm fearlessness, such as: *I am forever divinely guided and know I am always protected and safe. I fear nothing and no one. Fearlessness is mine.* Don't be afraid to spice your affirmations with zeal, and avoid empty, parrot-like repetitions for best results. Repeat your favourite affirmations daily and as often as you wish. Remember, there is nothing to fear.

Dare To Dream

ORACLE OBSERVATIONS: SEVEN
FROM WITHIN TO WITHOUT

Meditate. Get a rest from the mind chatter.

A little quiet time, a moment of silence, will do wonders for you. Meditation gives you the opportunity to get away from the mind-babble, to quiet down, throw off negative thoughts and purify old, accumulated toxic feelings. A hiatus, if you will, from the endless chatter going on in your head.

Meditation provides an oasis, a refuge from the outside world and a point in time, to get in touch with you in order to nourish your body, mind, and spirit. A moment of silence to focus, regroup and infuse your being with the needed vital energies that will give you the strength and courage to face the challenges at hand.

If you decide to give meditation a try, make sure you keep things simple and easy. No need for hocus-

pocus drama, like wrapping your head in exotic turbans, humming hymns or assuming difficult acrobatic poses. All you require is a comfortable place to sit, whatever suits you best, and remember to keep your spine in an upright position. Close your eyes, relax and keep your focus centered on the bridge of your nose. The goal is to quiet your thoughts. Keep the focus and refrain from going over your grocery shopping list or the bills you forgot to pay or how you're going to give a piece of your mind to what's-her-face. Think of meditation as your out-of-the-ordinary time, your get-in-touch-with-yourself spa.

You can meditate in the morning and upon retiring at night for about fifteen minutes maximum. Remember, less is more. The important thing is that you be steadfast and meditate everyday. The benefits of meditation are numerous. Watch for improved relationships, expect a calmer attitude to what is going on around you, worry less, look for enhanced sleep,

and enjoy a healthier life.

Your inner sanctum awaits you with all the breathtaking benefits it has to offer. Enter and discover yourself. Link up, connect to the vital source and gradually augment your self-awareness while stoking the fires of self-knowledge. Keep in mind, meditation is not a luxury—it's a must.

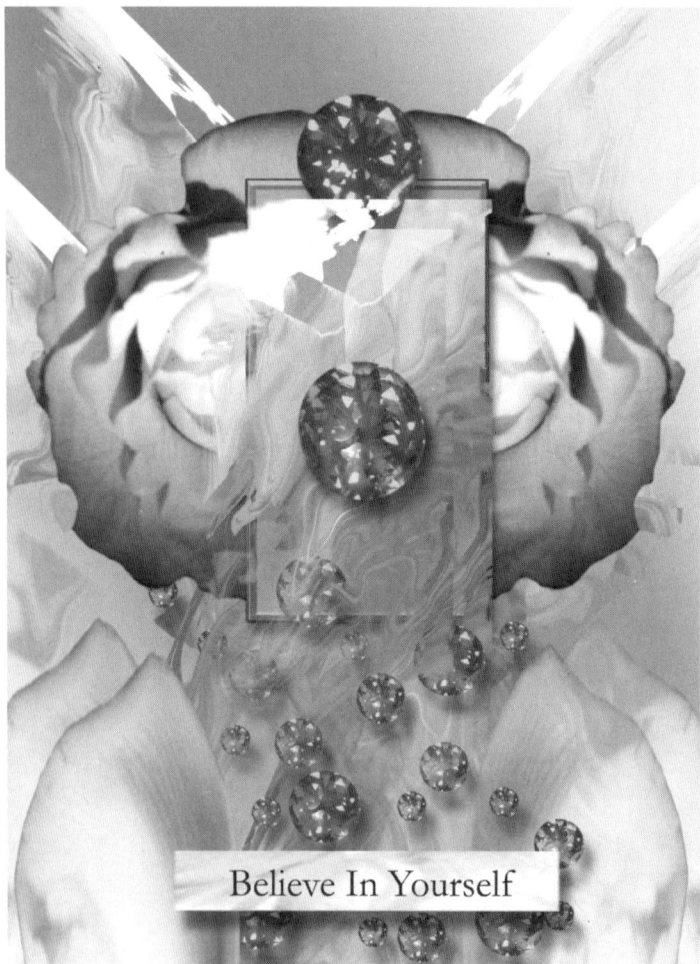
Believe In Yourself

THE AUTHOR

ORDER FORM

Please send *The Electric Oracle Speaks* to:

Name   _____

Address _____

City _____ Province/State _____

Postal or Zip Code _____

Country _____

Telephone _____

Email   _____

Price $14.95 Can./$11.95 US

Number of copies   _____

Shipping and handling $9.00 (all destinations)
For each additional copy add $5.00   _____

Total   _____

Please mail cheque or money order to:

daPress
599-B Yonge St., Suite 221
Toronto, Ontario, Canada M4Y 1Z4

Make check or money order payable to Rolland E. Proulx.

Allow 3 to 4 weeks for delivery.

If you wish to make a credit card payment via PayPal, please visit
www.rollandproulx.com